Learning Centers for
Advent and Lent

LEARNING CENTERS *for*
Advent and Lent

Doris Murphy

TWENTY
THIRD 23rd
PUBLICATIONS

Twenty-Third Publications
A Division of Bayard
One Montauk Avenue, Suite 200
New London, CT 06320
(860) 437-3012 or (800) 321-0411
www.23rdpublications.com

ISBN 978-1-58595-686-9

Library of Congress Catalog Card Number: 2008921776
Printed in the U.S.A.

Table of Contents

Learning Centers for Holy Week

Learning Centers for the Whole Community

Advent

Lent

Appendix

Introduction

Learning centers are one means for helping parents and other adults get involved in the religious formation of children in non-intimidating and practical ways. Many parents are eager to learn more about their own faith and want to hand that faith on to their children, but they don't feel they have adequate training or enough information to do so. Yet parents share their faith best through example, family rituals, and conversations. Learning centers can help them extend this process. This practical method of faith sharing can be used with almost any doctrinal content when presented in an age-appropriate manner with sensitivity to various learning styles.

So here parents are provided the opportunity to complete hands-on tasks, have discussions/ conversations about their faith with their children, and reinforce material that is addressed in their children's textbooks.

Learning centers offer creative and interactive ways to do this. Plus they are flexible. Parents can choose a convenient time to visit the center with their children and work at their own pace. It usually takes about two hours to thoughtfully visit the sessions and complete the activities. Learning centers also give the director of faith formation an opportunity to observe parents, children, and other adults working together. This can help him or her determine which learning centers are most beneficial in the learning process.

A few practical points:

- If possible, before families visit the individual learning centers, review briefly with them the sheet of directions they will find at each center, which list the church teaching, the goal of the activity, and directions.

- Make copies of the short suggested readings from the *Catechism of the Catholic Church* and have them at the appropriate centers so those who wish can read them.

- Make certain that each center has all the supplies needed and enough of each supply.

- At each center have a Bible with a marker on the page where the appropriate passage for that center can be easily found. (You might want to use a child's version of the Bible for these readings.)

Special thanks to Carol Mercord, Religious Education Director at St. Joseph Parish in Prescott, Wisconsin, who continues to give her support, help, and advice in developing these centers.

Also thanks to Diane Wengelski at St. Bridget's Parish for her suggestions about how to use the learning centers.

And special thanks to my nephew Nathan for his computer savvy.

Learning Centers for
Advent

The Jesse Tree

Church Teaching

Catechism of the Catholic Church, paragraphs 64, 712

Goals

To prepare with hope for the coming of Jesus
To understand that the Jesse Tree is the family tree of Jesus
To learn about the ancestors of Jesus
To appreciate your own family tree and your own relatives

Supplies

Bible
Envelope with slips of names for Jesse Tree symbols
Sheet for your own family tree
Glue, colored paper, scissors, pencils, crayons, art materials
Pieces of yarn; paper punch
A tree branch or small Christmas tree

Directions for Activities

• Read Matthew 1:1–17, Jeremiah 33:15, Acts of the Apostles 13:22–23.

• Talk about your own family tree. Write the names of your ancestors on the paper provided.

• Discuss the meaning of the Jesse Tree.

The Jesse Tree

Our ancestors, the people in our family tree, are often unique and interesting. The people who make up our "faith family," ones who show us how we are related to Jesus, are also unique and interesting. For example, the Bible tells us that Jesus was the relative of David, Israel's greatest king, and he was also related to Abraham, an early leader of the Hebrew people. Through these and many other faithful people, God took flesh as Jesus and lived among us.

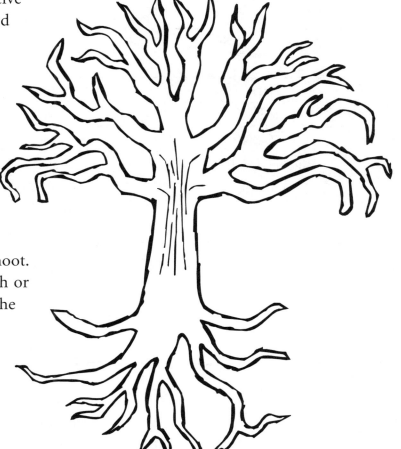

The Jesse Tree is Jesus' family tree. Jesse was the father of King David, and Isaiah wrote that a shoot (a branch) would come forth from the root of Jesse, meaning that Jesus would be this shoot. A Jesse Tree, made with a bare branch or small tree, holds symbols of some of the people from the Old Testament who waited and prepared for Jesus. It is an Advent custom to think about and pray to Jesus' ancestors.

- Draw one strip from the envelope. Make the symbol of that person as suggested. Use some of the art materials.

- When finished, put a piece of string on the symbol and hang it on the tree.

- Take a list of the Jesse Tree names home with you. Make a different symbol for each day of Advent and hang it on a tree (branch) at home as you wait for Christmas. Read the assigned Scripture story for each symbol as well.

Note to Facilitator: When all have completed their symbols, place the tree where all can enjoy it during the Advent season.

Symbols for the Jesse Tree

Adam and Eve	tree of good and evil	Genesis 3:1–24
	fruit (apple)	Genesis 3:1–24
Noah	ark, boat	Genesis 6:13–17
	rainbow	Genesis 9:8–17
	animals	Genesis 6:17–22; 7:1–4
Abraham and Sarah	tent	Genesis 12:8–9
Abraham	stars	Genesis 15:5–7
Isaac	ram	Genesis 22:1–14
Rebecca	a well	Genesis 24:12–21
Jacob	ladder	Genesis 28:10–17
Rachel and Leah	baskets	Genesis 29:15–30
Joseph	coat of colors	Genesis 37:1–4
Moses	burning bush	Exodus 3:1–15
	Ten Commandments	Exodus 20:1–21
Rahab	red rope	Joshua 2:1–21
Deborah	palm tree	Judges 4:4–7
Gideon	torch	Judges 7:16–18
Sampson	jawbone	Judges 15:14–17
Ruth	stalk of wheat	Ruth, Chapters 1—4
Samuel	oil	1 Samuel 16:1–13
David	stringed harp	1 Samuel 16:14–23
	slingshot	1 Samuel 17:42–58
Solomon	crown	1 Kings 3:4–14
	temple	1 Kings 6:4–14
Elijah	chariot	2 Kings 2:9–14
Jonah	whale	Jonah 2:1–10
Isaiah	root/branch	Isaiah 11:1–9
Ezekiel	bones	Ezekiel 37:1–14
Daniel	lion	Daniel 6:10–23
Elizabeth	home	Luke 1:39–45
John the Baptist	shell and water	Matthew 3:4–12
Joseph	hammer and saw	Matthew 1:19–21
Mary	manger	Luke 2:1–14

Our Family Tree

Who is in your family now? Who is the oldest person you know about who is related to you? Why does it matter to know your relatives? How would you feel if you found out that one of your relatives was a king or a queen? Is it important that your relatives would be people of justice? What does that mean?

These are the people in my family:

My Name _____

Other People in My Family:

_____

_____

_____

_____

_____

_____

_____

_____

_____

_____

The O Antiphons

Church Teaching

Catechism of the Catholic Church, paragraphs 452, 2648

Goals

To know the importance and meaning of the O Antiphons

To learn the many different names used for Jesus (especially "God with us")

To celebrate Advent in our homes with special prayers

Supplies

Bible

Copy of the song "O Come, O Come Emmanuel"

Sheet of circles for the O Antiphons

Pencils, crayons, markers

Prayer sheet

Directions for Activities

• Read Isaiah 9:6 and Matthew 1:22–23.

• Explain the meaning of the O Antiphons: Antiphons are short prayers that are prayed when people come together for evening prayer (also called vespers). Seven days before Christmas, the O Antiphons are sung. Each begins with the word "O," followed by a different name for Jesus.

• Take the sheet with seven circles and prayers on the other side. Each of these is an "O." Draw a picture inside the "O" that shows a symbol of the Jesus-name.

   1. O Wisdom—an eye

   2. O Adonai—hand

   3. O Root of Jesse—tree root

   4. O Key of David—key

   5. O Rising Dawn—rising sun

   6. O King of Nations—crown

   7. O Emmanuel, God-with-us—crib/manger

The O Antiphons

Pray an O Antiphon each evening from December 18 to December 24. Let each remind you to open your heart to Jesus as you prepare for Christmas.

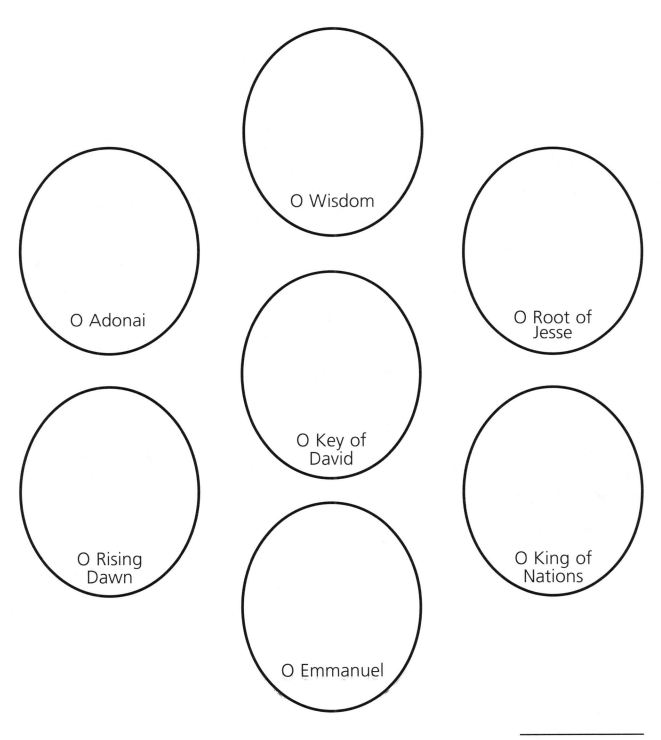

O Wisdom

O Adonai

O Root of Jesse

O Key of David

O Rising Dawn

O King of Nations

O Emmanuel

O Wisdom, come and teach us the way of the Lord

O Adonai, leader of Israel, come to save us with an outstretched hand

O Root of Jesse, come to save us and don't delay

O Key of David, come open the way and lead us out of darkness

O Rising Dawn, come to bring us light

O King of Nations, come and save us whom you made out of dust

O Emmanuel, God-with-us, come and save us, O Lord, our God

The Church Year

Church Teaching

Catechism of the Catholic Church, paragraphs 524, 1168–1173

Goals

To learn the meaning of the term "church year" or "liturgical year"
To name the different seasons of the church year that celebrate events in the life of Jesus
To learn why different colors are used during the church year
To experience that "time" is holy

Supplies

Bible
Circle/calendar of the church year
Crayons, scissors
Brads for spinner
"Church Year" information sheets
Refrigerator calendar

Directions for Activities

• Read Exodus 23:14–19 or Deuteronomy 16:1–17.

• Cut out the circular calendar and spinner. Color the sections of the calendar as indicated (between the dotted lines).

• Use a brad to make the spinner; mark the seasons when they occur through the year.

• Discuss the information on "The Church Year" sheet.

• Take one of the calendars to place on your refrigerator or door and write the dates when Advent begins and ends. On each date write something you are doing to prepare for Christmas, for example: call or write family friends you have not seen for a while; donate a package of socks to a homeless shelter; play a game with your family; read a book instead of watching TV; as a family, visit someone in a nursing home; pray for peace throughout our world; work together to clean your room and the whole house; make an ornament for your Christmas tree; wrap a gift for someone at a shelter.

The Church Year

Celebrating the liturgical or church year is one of the ways Christians have to make "time" holy or sacred. The events of the liturgical year tell the entire story of the life of Jesus and remind us that Jesus is still with us. As with the calendar year, the liturgical year is a way we can measure time.

The most important feast of the church year is Easter, which is preceded by the **Triduum** (three days), which begins on **Holy Thursday** and ends with **Easter**. On Easter we celebrate the Resurrection of the Lord. The colors of Easter are white or gold, and the priest's clothing (vestments) reflect this.

We prepare for Easter throughout the forty days of **Lent** and the color for this season is purple, a sign of penance.

The Easter season lasts for fifty days and ends with **Pentecost**, the feast on which we celebrate the presence of the Holy Spirit in our hearts and in our church. The color for Pentecost is red.

Another important feast is **Christmas**, when we remember and celebrate the birth of Jesus. The priest wears wears white or gold for this celebration.

We prepare for Christmas throughout the four weeks of **Advent**. Advent is a time of waiting for Jesus who is our Emmanuel: God-with-us. Here the color is purple.

The time between these seasons is called **Ordinary Time**. On the Sundays of Ordinary Time, we learn from the gospel stories about Jesus and what he taught. The color for this season is green.

During the liturgical year we also celebrate the feasts of **saints**—those who followed the gospel and were close to God during their lives.

The following symbols are used during the liturgical year:

Advent: a wreath with four candles—three are purple, one is pink
Christmas: star and crib—white
Lent: cross—purple
Easter: lily or white cloth—white or gold
Pentecost: dove or flames—red
Ordinary Time: vine and branches—green

Church Year Calendar

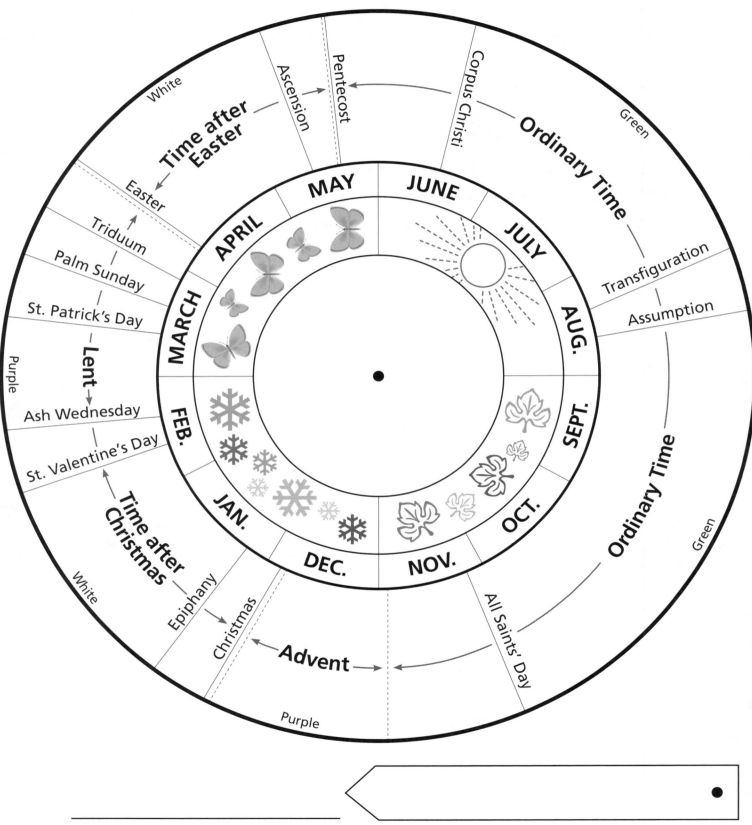

Refrigerator Calendar

Sunday	Monday	Tuesday	Wednesday	Thursday	Friday	Saturday

Prepare the Way for Jesus

Church Teaching

Catechism of the Catholic Church, paragraphs 523, 608, 717–720

Goals

To understand we can be signs of Jesus for others
To learn from John the Baptist (cousin of Jesus who showed us the way to Jesus)
To speak out about what Jesus calls us to do and to be
To discover which actions show us the way to Jesus

Supplies

Bible
Sheet of stones to make a road
Glue, scissors, crayons
Sheet to make a path
Prayer sheet

Directions for Activities

• Read Matthew 3:1–6.

• The cousin of Jesus was John the Baptist (son of Elizabeth and Zachary). His work was to prepare the way for Jesus. John the Baptist reminds us to "fill every valley and level every mountain" in our lives to prepare the way for Jesus. What are some hills and valleys in your life?

• Read the messages on the stepping stones. Cut out or color only the ones that describe good actions. Paste them on a sheet to make a straight path to Jesus.

• Pray together:

Leader   Jesus calls us to feed the hungry
All   Help us to be a sign for others.

Leader	Jesus calls us to visit the sick
All	Help us to be a sign for others.
Leader	Jesus calls us to visit those in prison
All	Help us to be a sign for others.
Leader	Jesus calls us to give drink to the thirsty
All	Help us to be a sign for others.
Leader	Jesus calls us to give shelter to the homeless
All	Help us to be a sign for others.
Leader	Jesus calls us to clothe the naked
All	Help us to be a sign for others.
Leader	Jesus, please help us to be signs of your love in our world.
All	Help us to be a sign for others.

How are you now doing these things as a family? How might you do them better?

Which stones make a straight path?

Jesus tells us that some signs of the kingdom of God are peace, love, joy, and holiness. Jesus himself was a sign of God's kingdom here on earth. As we prepare for Christmas, we too can do good things for one another and thus be signs of God's love.

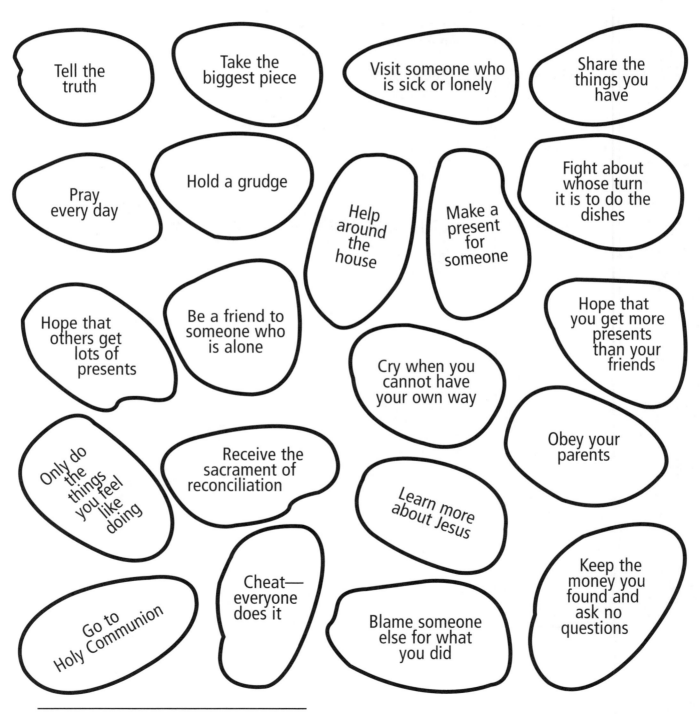

Be Watchful and Patient

Church Teaching

Catechism of the Catholic Church, paragraphs 522, 671

Goals

To do good things for family members throughout Advent

To experience the importance of waiting

To practice patience as we prepare our hearts and homes for Christmas

Supplies

Bible

Sheets of green and red strips with suggested actions for each day
    (divided into the two colors)

Glue, scissors

Discussion questions

Directions for Activities

• Read James 5:7–10 and Mark 13:33–37.

• Discuss the following questions:

   » What might you miss during Advent if you are not watchful?

   » What is it like when you are watching and waiting for a loved one to come ? How is this like waiting for Jesus?

   » What are some things you do while you wait for Jesus?

• Cut apart the red and green strips. Make a long paper chain by gluing the alternate colors in loops together. The final loop is for Christmas Day.

• Be patient! Take the chain home. Each day until Christmas take off one loop and do the action suggested on the slip.

Actions for the Green and Red Strips

Write a Christmas letter to someone.

Put up some Christmas decorations; get out the Christmas crib.

Draw a picture of someone waiting for something special.

Make a Christmas poster this week.

Help clean the house.

Tell or write a story about preparing for Christmas. Share the story with someone else.

Think quietly for a few minutes about the people you love.

Help bake Christmas cookies; take some to a neighbor.

Give away one of your best smiles.

Call or write your grandmother or grandfather today.

Reflect for a few minutes and then list some gifts you have already received in your life.

Make or wrap some presents.

Write down or draw three things you hope for. Talk about these with someone.

Say "I'm sorry" to someone you have hurt.

Do something for your mom or dad without being asked.

Start a family discussion with the question: What does Advent mean to me?

Offer to help an older neighbor with an odd job.

Pray today for those who are lonely.

Send a note or an email to a relative.

Take time to compliment your parish pastor on the homily.

Draw a picture of the stable in Bethlehem where Jesus was born.

Forgive someone who has hurt you.

Family discussion: Why is Christmas worth waiting for? Why is waiting part of life?

Thank God for your family. Tell each person in your family why you appreciate them.

Rejoice and give thanks for Christmas.

Presents and Presence

Church Teaching

Catechism of the Catholic Church, paragraphs 1095, 1999

Goals

To reflect on Christmas as a time when Jesus is present to us: in the story of Bethlehem; in the Eucharist; in one another

To keep Christmas as a time for giving and doing things for others

To witness the presence of Jesus in people whose lives show love, justice, and forgiveness

Supplies

Bible

Sheet to list presents for yourself, family, friends, and the world

Pencils, markers, crayons

Directions for Activities

- Read Luke 3:10–11.

- Discuss the questions on the following page.

- Take a copy of the sheet with the boxes for yourself, a special friend, family, and world neighbors. In each box, write some things you could give to each of these groups. Color the ribbon.

- Did you include any of these gifts in your lists?

  » Make your own candles or handiwork (art, sewing, etc.)

  » Give a plant and tell how to care for it.

  » Offer your services for babysitting, cleaning, mowing, getting groceries, shoveling snow.

  » Give of your talents through a poem, song, dance, or story.

  » Visit someone needy each week.

Discussion Questions

How are you getting ready for Christmas? What plans are you making?

Will you have company in your home or go to visit others?

In your family, is Christmas more about giving or receiving?

How are presents a sign of the Christmas season? What do they represent?

Can you think of "alternative" gifts (making them instead of buying them)?

In what ways does your family life give witness to the presence of Jesus?

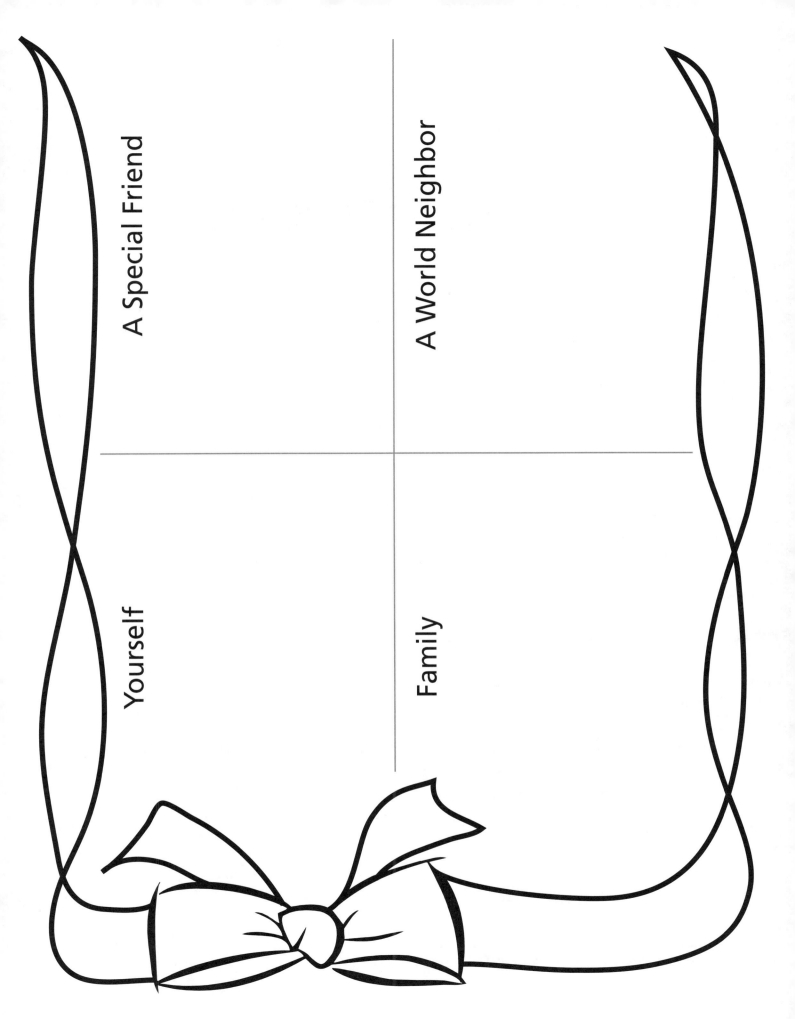

A Special Friend

A World Neighbor

Yourself

Family

Names for Jesus

Church Teaching

Catechism of the Catholic Church, paragraphs 430, 436, 454

Goals

To learn about some of the names for Jesus
To learn more about the life of Jesus
To understand why the gospel is called Good News
To make a Chi-Rho (ke-row), a sign for Jesus

Supplies

Bible
Slips of paper for Chi-Rho
Pencils, colors, scissors, glue
Paper punch, string, glitter
"Making a Chi-Rho" sheet
Word Find sheet
Sheet with names for Jesus and puzzle

Directions for Activities

• Read Matthew 1:20–21 and Romans 10:6.

• Together make a Chi-Rho following the instructions on the "Make a Chi-Rho" sheet.

• How many names for Jesus can you circle in the Word Find? See possibilities under the "Word List." After you find the names, ask your parent(s) to tell you what they mean.

• Can you figure out what the puzzle frame says?

Make a Chi-Rho

The Chi-Rho is a symbol made from the first two letters in Christ's name in Greek (Chi = X and Rho = P). You may have seen these letters on the communion host, on the priest's vestments, on prayer books, or somewhere in church.

- Take a square piece and a long rectangle and make the letter "P."

- Cross two short rectangles and make an "X."

- Paste the "X" over the length of the "P."

- Punch a hole and put a string in it to place the Chi-Rho on your tree; decorate it with some glitter.

Names of Jesus Word Find

```
A E J N D A O K F B L
P M C H R I S T D H A
R A E J O Q R K A F M
I S I U L Z G I A V B
N T B F K N S C F T O
C E L S T S U X R M F
E R E D E E M E R B G
O V A M Q D C W A H O
F Z D P J H J Y B G D
P S K I E L N F B C O
E O E M P S A V I O R
A M W D O Y P I E X N
C I T E A C H E R L H
E C G L P B G C M H D
```

Word List

CHRIST
The anointed one of God

LAMB OF GOD
One offered to God as a sacrifice

LORD
One having power and authority

MASTER
A revered religious leader

MESSIAH
The expected king and deliverer

PRINCE OF PEACE
The ruler of a peaceful kingdom

RABBI
A master teacher of Jewish law, the Hebrew word for teacher of God's word

REDEEMER
A person who redeems or saves others

SAVIOR
One who brings salvation and saves others

TEACHER
One who instructs others

What Do You See?

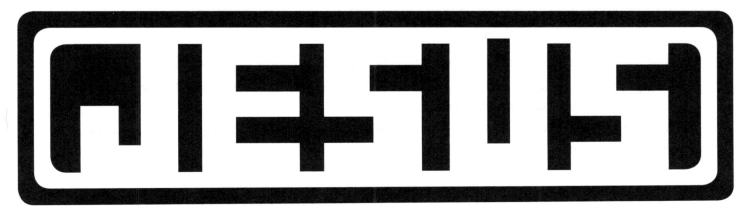

Hail Mary

Hail Mary, full of grace,
the Lord is with you.
Blessed are you among women, and
blessed is the fruit of your womb,
Jesus.
Holy Mary, Mother of God,
pray for us sinners, now
and at the hour of our death.
Amen.

Magnificat

My heart praises you, Lord, my soul is glad because of God my Savior.
For you have remembered me, your lowly servant!
From now on all people will call me blessed because of the
great things that you have done for me.
Your name is holy; from one generation to another,
You show mercy to those who honor you.
You have scattered the proud with all their plans.
You have brought down the mighty kings from their thrones,
and lifted up the lowly,
filled the hungry with good things,
and sent the rich away with empty hands.
You have kept the promise made to our ancestors,
and have come to the help of Israel.
You have remembered to show mercy to Abraham
and to all his descendants forever!

St. Joseph

Church Teaching

Catechism of the Catholic Church, paragraphs 532, 1846

Goals

To meet St. Joseph as the foster-father and the caregiver of Jesus and the husband of Mary

To learn that Jesus came to earth as one of us

To listen when God speaks to us in prayer and through others

Supplies

Bible

Brown paper to make a crib

Pieces of yellow paper

Scissors and glue

Matching sheet

Direction for Activities

- Read Matthew 1:18–24.

- Since a stable was the only room for the Holy Family, Joseph probably made the manger-crib as ready as he could. Cut out the crib model and fold and paste it as directed.

- Cut some yellow strips for straw; each day as you get ready for Jesus put a piece of straw in the crib. If you have a crèche at home, help get it ready. Perhaps put one figure in each day—finally placing Jesus in the crib on Christmas Eve.

- Match the columns on the sheet to see how much you know about Christmas.

What do you know about Christmas?
Matching Game

1. Joseph   Mother of Jesus

2. Mary   King who wanted Jesus killed

3. Shepherds   Angel who visited Mary

4. John the Baptist   Led Magi to Jesus

5. Nativity   Heard about Jesus from the angels

6. Magi   Town where Jesus was born

7. Bethlehem   Followed the star

8. Star   Husband of Mary

9. Herod   Birth of Jesus

10. Gabriel   Cousin of Jesus

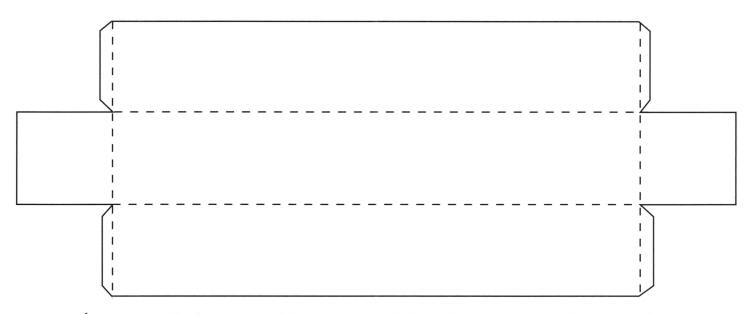

(Cut the solid lines and fold the dotted lines. Then paste to form a crib!)

A Special Christmas Card

Church Teaching

Catechism of the Catholic Church, paragraphs 456, 525

Goals

To think about how Mary and Joseph prepared for the coming of Jesus

To wait with others during the days of Advent for the Lord to come into our hearts

To make a Christmas card for your parents

Supplies

Bible

Black or blue sheet of construction paper

Figures of Mary, Joseph, Jesus, star

Glue, scissors, pencils

Lined paper for letter

Directions for Activities

- Read Luke 2:1–7 and Romans 13:11–14.

- Take a piece of blue or black paper and fold it in half.

- Cut out the figures from the sheet (Mary, Joseph, Jesus, star) and paste them on the front of the folded paper.

- Paste a piece of lined paper inside. Write a Christmas note and give this to your parent(s) as a gift.

Figure Patterns

Bethlehem

Church Teaching

Catechism of the Catholic Church, paragraphs 525, 544

Goals

To learn that Bethlehem means "House of Bread"
To find Bethlehem on a map or globe—as a place where there is little peace now
To imagine what it was like for Mary and Joseph to go on the trip to Bethlehem
To practice meditation

Supplies

Bible
Meditation sheet
Soft pillows and low lamp light
A space for meditation
Globe or map

Directions for Activities

• Parent: Read the meditation slowly and gently to your child(ren).

• When finished, keep a moment of silence or talk about the experience of a "visit" with Mary and Joseph.

• Find Bethlehem on a globe or map. What do you know about that part of the world?

Meditation

"One Starry Night in Bethlehem"

(Have children sit quietly as an adult begins to read slowly)

Mary and Joseph must have been very excited about the coming birth of their baby…

Joseph probably made a special crib. Mary probably spent some time making baby clothes. But something happened to upset their plans. The emperor ordered that a census had to be taken. All had to go to their hometowns to register their names so they could be counted. Mary and Joseph had to travel a long way to Bethlehem. It was not a good time to travel but they had to go…

We are going to be with Mary and Joseph as they arrive in Bethlehem. Close your eyes. Take a deep breath and relax. It is evening and you are in the very crowded town of Bethlehem…

Joseph leads the donkey through the streets. Mary is seated on the donkey. It has been a long, hard journey and they are very tired. Mary is worried because her baby is coming soon. Joseph is looking for a place to sleep but he has not been able to find one. You are standing with Joseph and Mary in front of the last place to look. He is afraid there is no room left. People are pushing and shoving. A servant comes out and says, "There is no room here." But he is kind and smiles at you and says, "I will show you a place where you can at least find some rest." Joseph walks beside the donkey and Mary and you follow along. The servant takes you to a stable. He makes a bed out of the hay. Joseph helps Mary off the donkey. You watch Mary lie down on the fresh hay. Joseph asks you to make sure the animals have hay. You know God will take care of everything. Then you hear a baby's cry and you know Jesus has come…

Mary looks very tired and the baby is in her arms. Joseph is sitting next to Mary. He wants to make sure she is feeling okay. Joseph smiles. You and Joseph watch Mary and the baby Jesus. You feel very happy to be so close to Jesus in your mind and heart…

What are you thinking? Pray in your heart: "I love you, Jesus. Thank you for coming into this world. Thank you for loving me and everyone. Mary, thank you for saying yes when God asked you to be the mother of his Son. Thank you, Joseph, for taking care of Mary and Jesus."

Advent/Christmas Video

Church Teaching

Catechism of the Catholic Church, paragraphs 2444, 2447

Goals

To review the Christmas story

To imagine how Christmas makes a difference in our lives

Supplies

DVD player and TV

The Angel's Advent Lesson or "Christian Crossroads" (episode 2 from *Following Jesus through the Church Year*)—both available from Twenty-Third Publications

Directions for Activity

- Watch the video alone or with others.
- When you are finished watching, complete the sentence:
    What I learned today about Christmas…
- Discuss these questions as a family.
    » What is Advent?
    » Why does the church have a special "waiting time" before Christmas?
    » What is your favorite thing about Advent?

Learning Centers for
Lent

The Cross

Church Teaching

Catechism of the Catholic Church, paragraphs 219, 571, 616

Goals

To understand the cross as a sign of God's love and forgiveness; Jesus gave everything for us

To make a cross you can keep in your home or room as one sign of being a Christian

To learn to make the sign of the cross with reverence

Supplies

Bible

Directions for making a cross

White paper

Scissors, markers, pencil, colored pencils

Sheet of various crosses

Direction for Activities

• Read John 3:16.

• Make a cross from the directions or choose a picture from the sheet of crosses and make one of those. Take the sheet home and see if you can find out more about those crosses from the Internet or an encyclopedia.

• Decorate the cross with markers. If desired, write on your cross: "God so loved the world that he sent us his only Son."

• Practice making the sign of the cross with reverence. Talk about what this sign means for us as Christians.

Paper Cross

Use 8½" x 11" paper. Fold along dotted lines as illustrated.

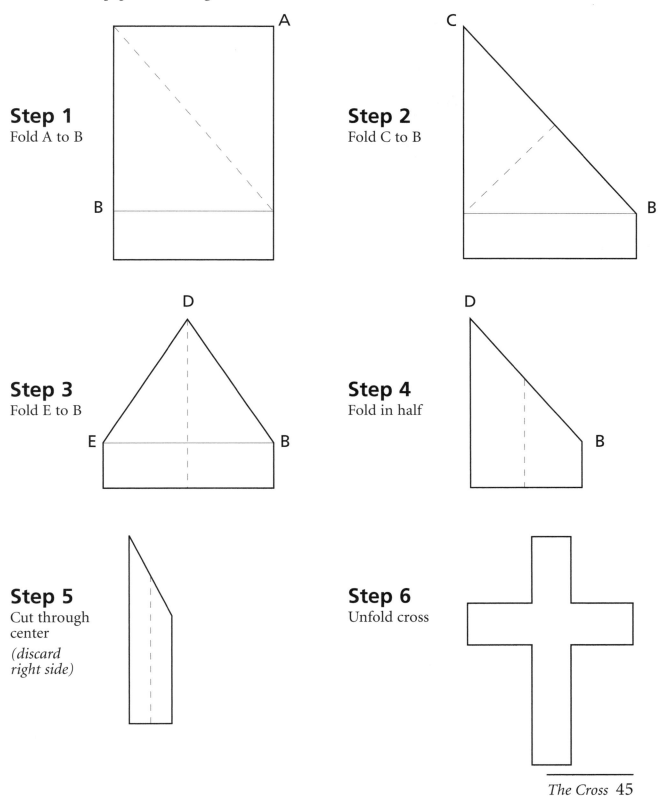

Step 1
Fold A to B

Step 2
Fold C to B

Step 3
Fold E to B

Step 4
Fold in half

Step 5
Cut through center

(discard right side)

Step 6
Unfold cross

Crosses

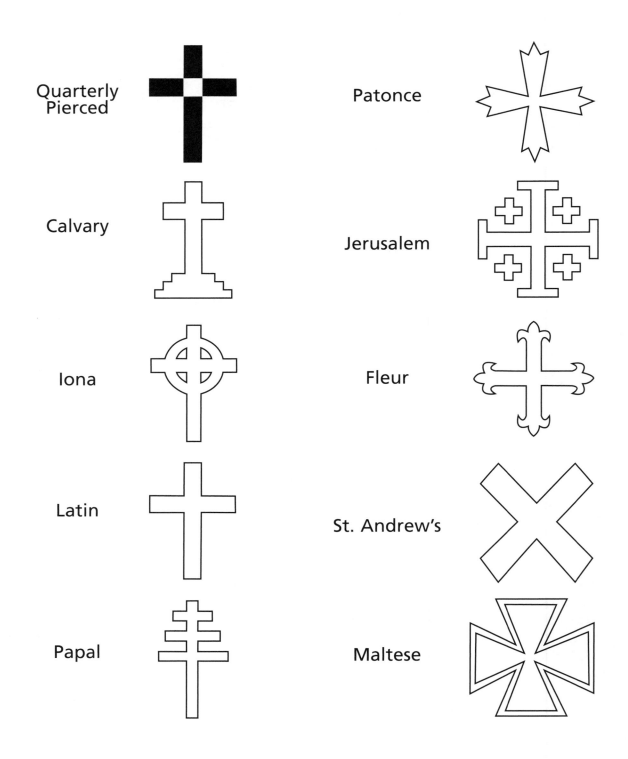

Quarterly Pierced

Calvary

Iona

Latin

Papal

Patonce

Jerusalem

Fleur

St. Andrew's

Maltese

Making Choices

Church Teaching

Catechism of the Catholic Church, paragraphs 2612, 2732, 2754

Goals

To understand Lent as forty days for growing in love of God

To make time in our lives to stop, pray, and act

To think about what is means to be captives to sin or to do things that do not give us life

To pray to our guardian angels to keep us from sin and danger

Supplies

Bible

Red, green, and yellow circles

Black markers, glue, scissors, pencils

White paper

Game sheet

Directions for Activities

- Read Mark 1:2–3 and John 8:1–11.

- Paste a red, yellow, and green circle on the white paper in the form of a stop light. Mark them: red-stop; yellow-pray; green-act; let this remind you to ask God's direction in your life.

- Take a game sheet covered with dots; the object of the game is to complete as many boxes as you can by connecting the dots. Draw only one line per each turn. The person who draws the final line of a box puts his or her initial in that box.

- After you have played the game, discuss the questions as a family.

- Pray together the Guardian Angel prayer.

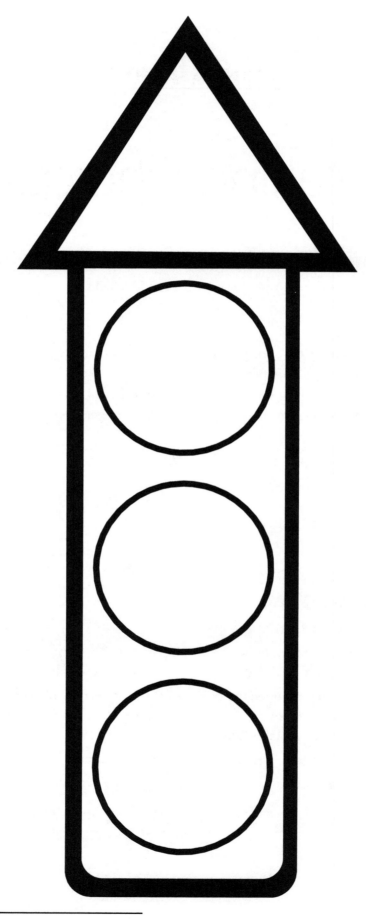

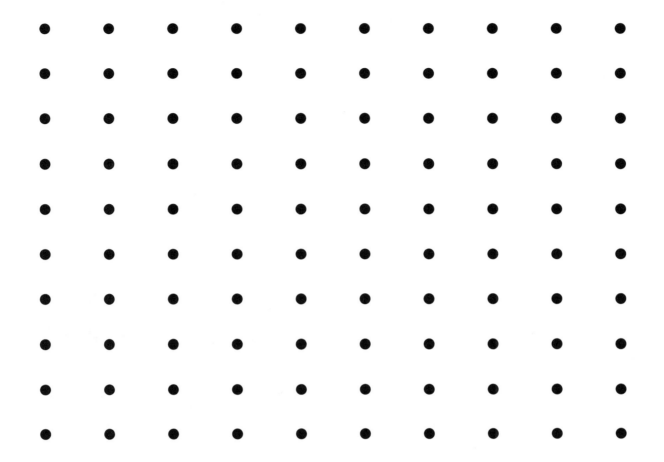

Discuss

Can you think of any other games where you have been trapped?

Can you think of real-life situations where you feel trapped?

If you have felt trapped, who has helped you out?

Have you ever tried to trap other people into doing things they did not want to do (manipulating, begging, making someone feel guilty or shameful, forcing others to go somewhere or do something they did not want to do)? What happened as a result?

Guardian Angel Prayer

Guardian angels help us when we are tempted, just as they helped Jesus when he was tempted. Angels are messengers from God. Pray the prayer to your guardian angel. Take a copy with you.

Angel of God
my guardian dear
To whom God's love
commits me here.
Ever this day be
at my side,
To light,
to guard,
to rule,
and guide.
Amen.

Keeping the Commandments

Church Teaching

Catechism of the Catholic Church, paragraphs 2052–2060

Goals

To review the Ten Commandments as God's Law

To discuss ways we "keep" or "break" each of the commandments

To keep the commandments as a lenten practice

Supplies

Bible

Pencils

Sheet about the Ten Commandments

Board game, one of a pair of dice, and game markers

Directions for Activities

- Read Exodus 20:1–7.

- Follow the directions on the Ten Commandment sheet.

- Play the board game. How can you keep or break the commandments? Shake the die and move your marker the correct number of spaces. If you land on a "Break" space, you must start over. See who finishes first and try to use the "Keep" suggestions during Lent.

The Ten Commandments

The Book of Exodus records that God gave Moses a set of ten commandments, or laws, by which the Israelites should live. In Jesus' day, these and other laws (called Mosaic law or the Law of Moses) were very important to Jews. Breaking one of these laws was considered a sin against God.

In Column 1, number the commandments the way you find them in the book of Exodus 20:1–17 (in the reading for the Third Sunday of Lent, Year B).

In Column 2, put a check beside the laws you think are important for you in your life now. What are some ways you **obey** these laws? What are some ways you **disobey** these laws?

Column 1   Column 2

_____   _____   Worship no God but me.

_____   _____   Do not use my name for evil purposes.

_____   _____   Observe the Sabbath and keep it holy.

_____   _____   Do not steal.

_____   _____   Do not commit murder.

_____   _____   Do not accuse anyone falsely.

_____   _____   Do not commit adultery.

_____   _____   Respect you father and your mother.

_____   _____   Do not desire another person's spouse.

_____   _____   Do not desire another person's property.

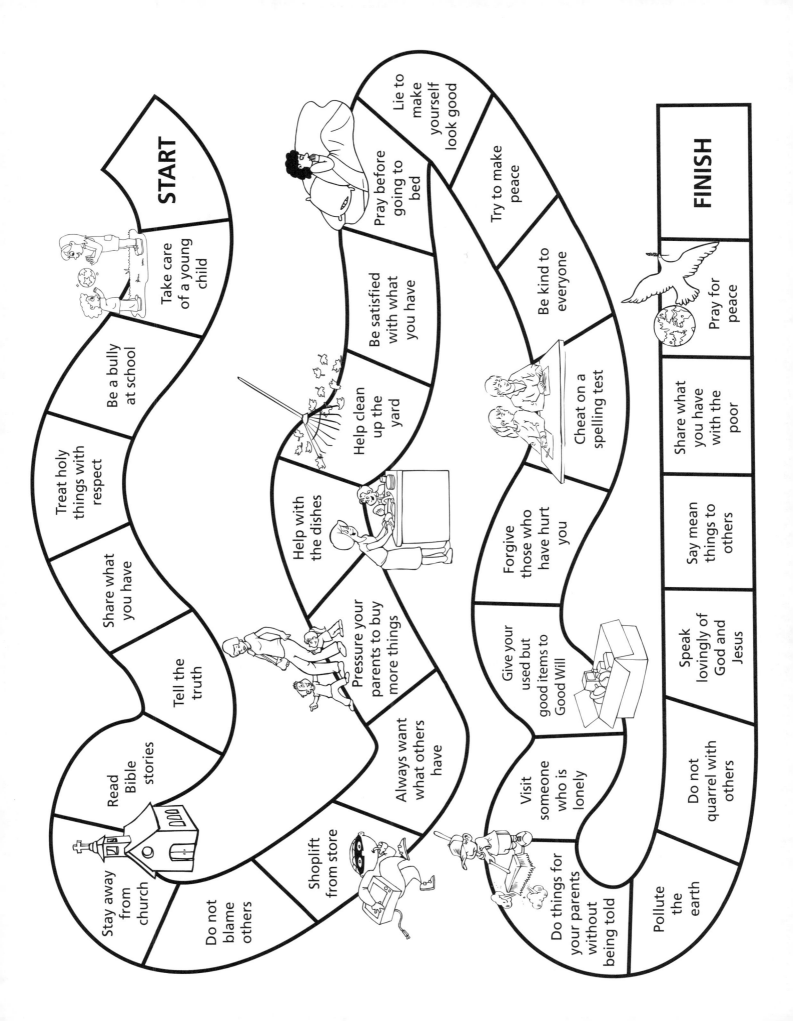

A Reminder of Prayer

Church Teaching

Catechism of the Catholic Church, paragraphs 2002, 2607

Goals

To learn about ways to pray during Lent: with praise and thanksgiving,
    to ask God's forgiveness, and to pray for our needs
To enjoy making pretzels, a traditional symbol of prayer during Lent

Supplies

Bible
Bread dough (½ of a refrigerator breadstick works well)
Parchment paper and small plastic bags
Explanation of the pretzel

Directions for Activities

• Read Mark 14:32–42.

• Discuss the various ways you can pray as a family: praise, thanksgiving, asking for forgiveness, and praying for our needs. Write a brief prayer in each prayer box on the "Ways to Pray" sheet.

• Read the explanation about lenten pretzels and follow the directions for making a pretzel.

• Take the pretzel home in the plastic bag to bake it—perhaps make some extras for the entire family.

Ways to Pray as a Family

Praise God

Give Thanks to God

Ask God's Forgiveness

Pray for Our Needs

What other ways can you pray as a family?

A Special Lenten Food

Perhaps the easiest and most significant lenten food custom is to serve a small pretzel to each family member with meals during Lent. The pretzel is a symbol of prayer and fasting.

The pretzel was the Christian lenten bread as far back as the fifth century. In the Roman Empire, the faithful Christians kept a strict fast all through Lent: no milk, butter, eggs, cheese, cream, or meat. They ate bread made of water, flour, and salt.

To remind themselves that Lent was a time of prayer, they shaped the bread into the form of arms crossed in prayer (in those days they crossed their arms over their chests while praying). They called the bread "little arms" (*bracellae*).

Today in many European places, pretzels are served only from Ash Wednesday to Easter, thus keeping the ancient symbolism alive.

Take a piece of dough (refrigerator breadsticks work well) and make a pretzel. Roll the dough into a rope-like shape. Bend the two ends around and cross one over the other. Pinch the dough together where the pieces meet. When you are finished, place your pretzel in a plastic bag and take it home for baking.

Lenten Practices

Church Teaching

Catechism of the Catholic Church, paragraphs 1430–1433

Goals

To understand that we are all tempted at times and that we can overcome temptation
    by prayer and good works
To respect quiet time for yourself and for others
To think of ways we can do lenten practices that follow in the gospel steps of Jesus

Supplies

Bible
Sheet of footsteps
Crayons, scissors
Doorknob hanger
Sheet of words
Envelopes

Directions for Activities

- Read Joel 2:12–16 and Matthew 4:1–10.

- Discuss: What is temptation; what does it mean to be tempted?

- Take a sheet of footsteps. On each step write something you can do to resist temptation. Prayer is one important way to spend time with God and to resist temptation.

- Color the doorknob hanger. Put it on your door when you want family members to know you would appreciate quiet time for prayer.

- Cut apart the sheet of words and put them into a "lenten practices" envelope. Decorate the envelope. Each day until Easter, select one word; spend a few minutes thinking and praying about it and then do something to practice it.

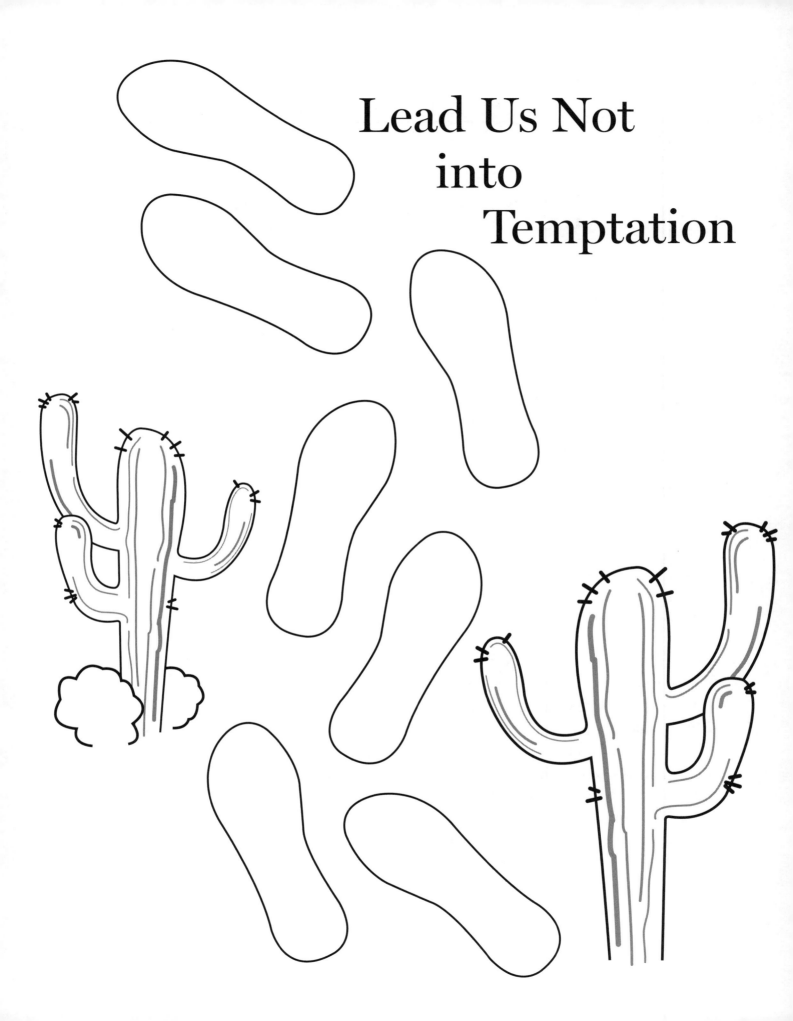

Lead Us Not into Temptation

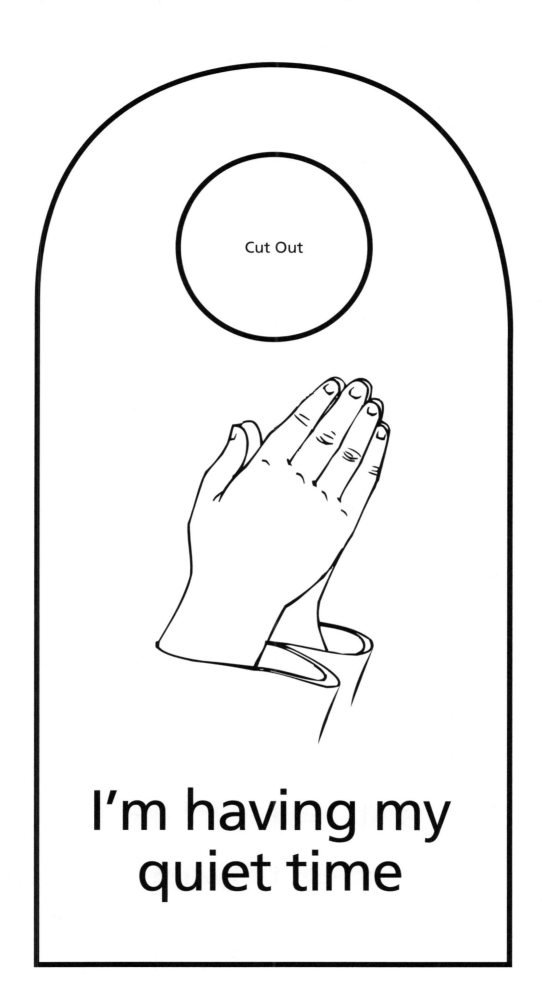

Trust	Love	Joy	Respect
Willingness	Courage	Friendship	Change
Care	Inspiration	Responsibility	Obey
Understanding	Patience	Faith	Hope
Communication	Creativity	Sharing	Justice
Freedom	Gratitude	Concern	Devotion
Forgiveness	Compassion	Goodness	Kindness
Truth	Peace	Generosity	Praise

A Holy Place

Church Teaching

Catechism of the Catholic Church, paragraphs 206, 210–211

Goals

To believe that God is a God of love and compassion

To learn about God's biblical name

To understand that where we stand is holy ground because God is present

Supplies

Bible

Scraps of colored paper to make a burning bush (red, yellow, gold, orange, brown, green, etc.)

Scissors, glue, crayons, pencils

Sheets of " I AM…"

Directions for Activities

• Read Exodus 3:1–15.

• On the sheet that says "I AM WHO I AM," take scraps of colored paper and make a burning bush.

• Beside the burning bush draw your shoes. This is a sign that where God is, is always a holy place—like our church or our home.

• Pray the Our Father together as a family.

And God spoke from the burning bush and said:

"I AM WHO I AM"

(in the Hebrew language this translates to the word "Yahweh.")

Our Need for Change

Church Teaching

Catechism of the Catholic Church, paragraphs 59, 72, 554–556

Goals

To learn how God transformed Abraham by making him the father of all nations (all believers)

To appreciate the reality that others have handed on our faith to us

To imagine how Jesus changed for his disciples and friends as they got to know him

Supplies

Bible

Discussion questions

Sheet of yellow stars and sheets of dark-colored paper

Pencils, scissors, paste, or glue

Pictures of faces

Directions for Activities

- Read Genesis 15:5–7 and Mark 9:2–10.

- Discuss the questions on the sheet. Cut out the stars and paste them on a sheet of the dark paper. How has it changed?

- On each star, write the name of an ancestor, a long-ago relative, who handed on the faith to you and your family.

- Take a sheet of the faces and go over the questions.

Discussion Questions

Abraham was called by God to be the father of the Jewish people. Abraham needed to be transformed, changed in some way, if he was going to follow the One God.

- How did God tell Abraham his life would change? How did Sarah's life change?

- What is meant by descendants?

God told Abraham that his descendants would number more than the stars in the heavens. On each star below, write the name of one of your ancestors who handed on your faith to you.

Faces

How does your face change in the course of a day?

How can your face be a face that shows kindness and love?

What do the faces below tell you about the kids?

How do you think Jesus' face looked on the mountain?

If you had been there, how would your own face have changed?

Jesus Blesses Us

Church Teaching

Catechism of the Catholic Church, paragraphs 1095, 1438, 1803

Goals

To rejoice that Jesus blesses us for our good deeds
To learn ways that we can follow Jesus more closely
To keep Lent as a time to offer blessings to others

Supplies

Bible
Sheet with balloons
"Blessings" sheet
Black markers

Directions for Activities

• Read Matthew 5:1–10.

• Take a balloon sheet and read the question on it. Talk about good qualities you already have and ways you can practice other good actions (virtues) during Lent.

• Together look at the "Our Family Has Blessings" sheet. Write in at least one good quality for each person named.

When Jesus spoke to the people in Matthew's gospel he blessed them for being poor in spirit, merciful, peacemakers, etc.

What good qualities or actions can Jesus bless you for? Color the balloons and write one of your good qualities in each balloon.

Our Family Has Blessings

Think about the good qualities of family members, friends, etc. and complete the blessings for each one. Add more names if you like.

Blessed is my father for he is _____
_____

Blessed is my mother for she is _____
_____

Blessed is my sister for she is _____
_____

Blessed is my brother for he is _____
_____

Blessed is my best friend for he/she is _____
_____

Blessed is my teacher for he/she is _____
_____

Blessed is my neighbor for he/she is _____
_____

Discuss
What blessing do you think Jesus would give you as a family?

Jesus Gives Life

Church Teaching

Catechism of the Catholic Church, paragraphs 638, 739, 2276

Goals

To recognize that all people will some day have new life with God

To give thanks for our friends as Jesus gave thanks for his friends

To reach out to people who are sick or lonely

Supplies

Bible

Sheets with two flowers

Poem "Promises"

White construction paper sheets

Scissors, glue, crayons

Directions for Activities

- Read John 11:21–27, 38–44.

- Discuss the following:

    » Read the poem "Promises." What promises do you make to others?

    » Martha felt alone when Lazarus died. When have you felt alone and abandoned?

    » Jesus comes to heal us and give us new life. How can you help people who need healing?

- Make a flower card to give it to someone who is sick or sad.

    » Fold a white sheet in half. Color the two flowers on the flower sheet.

    » Cut them out and glue them on the white sheet so the centers are together but the petals of one are between the petals of another. Draw the leaves and a stem.

    » Inside the card, write a letter to someone you know who is sad or ill and send it to them or print the poem "Promises."

Promises

There are promises that people make,
and much too often, people break.

There are promises the seasons bring,
summer to fall to winter to spring.

There are promises in nature's way
of creating beauty for every day.

There are promises of constant light,
in the morning sun and the moon at night.

As day is for play and night is for sleeping,
every promise is made for keeping.

And every word that God has spoken
is a promise that will not be broken.

—Unknown

Jesus Gives Us Light

Church Teaching

Catechism of the Catholic Church, paragraphs 958, 1816, 2616

Goals

To understand that Jesus healed a blind man and can "heal" us too

To learn how you can give light to others

To find ways to open your heart to others—as Jesus did

Supplies

Bible

Short story of Helen Keller with discussion questions

Scissors, glue

Heart puzzle pieces and plain paper sheets

Envelopes for the puzzle pieces

Directions for Activities

- Read John 9:1–7.

- Read the short passage about Helen Keller. Discuss the questions that follow the story.

- Empty from the envelope the heart pieces and read the good deeds on each piece.

- Take the pieces home with you and each day do one of the six good deeds for someone. At the end of each day paste and piece on a sheet of paper until you have completed the heart.

Helen Keller

Once there was a little girl named Helen Keller. When she was nineteen months old, after a sudden illness, she became deaf and blind. She grew up and lived to be an old lady. But during most of her life, she never saw the color of the sky or heard the wind blow. She couldn't see or hear a car when she crossed the street. Her eyes could not see; her ears could not hear. She learned to see and hear with her hands and heart.

Discussion

Can you imagine how the blind man in the gospel and Helen Keller felt?

Have you ever been in a dark place where seeing was difficult? How did it feel?

Do you believe that Jesus is the light of the world?

Do you believe that Jesus can show you how to give light to others? In what ways can you do this?

Sharing from the Heart

Share a toy or game with someone today.

Call an elderly relative to say hello.

Say please and thank you today.

Give "light" by smiling at everyone you meet today.

Help a classmate today.

Do something kind for your parents today.

We Have Living Water

Church Teaching

Catechism of the Catholic Church, paragraphs 1265–1267, 1427

Goals

To grow closer to Jesus by spending time in prayer
To think about ways we can be better people
To recall our baptism and what happened on that day

Supplies

Bible
Sheet of discussion questions
Picture of empty jug
Dish of "holy water"
Pencils

Directions for Activities

- Read John 4:5–42.

- Discuss the situations and questions on the sheet.

- Take one of the pictures of the empty jug. On the jug, write things for which you are thirsting (things in your life you need in order to be a better person).

- Bless yourself with holy water as you recall your baptism. (Your parents can help you with these memories.)

Discussion Questions

Sometimes we treat others unfairly (as the people in the gospel treated the Samaritan woman). What would you do in the following situations?

A family moves into your neighborhood. They do not speak English well and they have customs that may seem strange to you. Some parents have told their children not to play with the new children. Then one day, your new neighbors ask your family to come for a visit. *What will you do?*

You have just moved to a new school. There is a girl in your class who seems to have no friends at all. She dresses in clothes that are out of style. When you ask about her, the other kids tell you that her parents left her and she lives with her grandmother. Every day she walks home ahead of you—alone. One day she asks you to walk with her. You would like to walk with her, but you are afraid of what the other kids will say about you. *What will you do?*

You are a girl taking a class where you learn about cooking and sewing. There is one boy in your class. All the girls laugh at him, and the boys make fun of him for taking the class. But he is very good at cooking and sewing. *How do you feel about him?*

• Is there a part of your life that needs "living water" from Jesus?

• If you could talk to Jesus right now, what would you say to him?

• What do you think Jesus would say to you?

I am thirsting for...

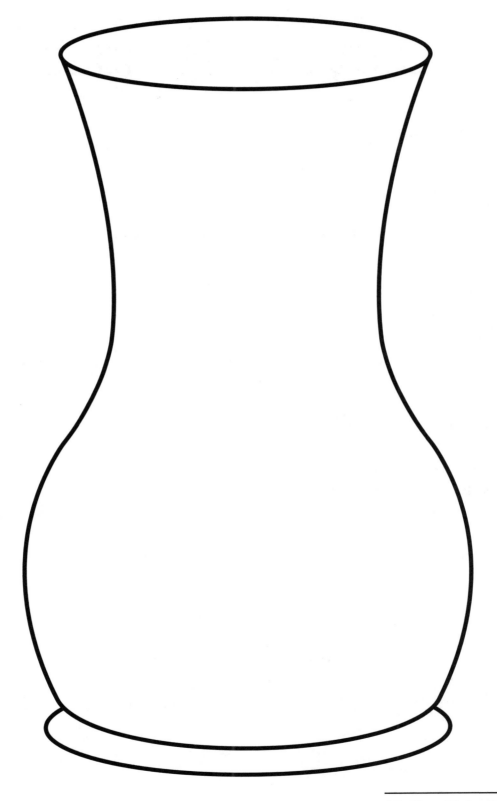

Lent/Easter Video

Church Teaching

Catechism of the Catholic Church, paragraphs 1095, 1168–1169, 1438

Goal

To understand that Lent is a time of preparation for the Triduum (three final days of Holy Week) and Easter

Supplies

DVD or VCR player

TV

Video *The Legend of the Three Trees* (Thomas Nelson, Inc.)
or *The Angel's Lenten Lesson* (Twenty-Third Publications)

Directions for Activities

- Together watch the video.
- Discuss the questions below:
  - » How long is Lent? (forty days)
  - » What happens on Palm Sunday? (all are given palm branches to recall the entry of Jesus into Jerusalem)
  - » What happens on Ash Wednesday? (Lent begins; all receive ashes on their forehead as a reminder that Lent is a time to change our ways)
  - » What are the Stations of the Cross? (a devotion that recalls Jesus' journey to Calvary)
  - » What happened on Holy Thursday? (Jesus celebrated a remembrance meal with his disciples)
  - » What happened on Good Friday? (Jesus died on the cross)
  - » How can you share with the poor during Lent?
  - » Do you receive the sacrament of reconciliation during Lent?

Learning Centers for
Holy Week

Symbols of Lent

Church Teaching

Catechism of the Catholic Church, paragraphs 612, 642

Goals

To study symbols that help us understand what happened to Jesus

To learn the meaning of various lenten symbols

Supplies

Bible

Pictures and explanation of symbols

Sheet for matching

Lenten game

Crayons

Directions for Activities

- Read the Passion Story of the Gospels (Mark 15:6–41).

- Game #1: Match word and symbol: answer the question by drawing a circle around the picture.

- Game #2 : Play the Lenten Cross Game following directions on the sheet.

Symbols of Lent

Number of days of Lent

Used to win the cloak of Jesus

Sign above the cross: Jesus of Nazareth, King of the Jews

Contained forty pieces of silver

Signs of Resurrection

Symbols of Communion

How Jesus was put on the cross

Children waved these to welcome Jesus

Color of the cloak they put on Jesus

Soldiers put this on Jesus' head to mock him as king

Jesus washed feet of disciples with this

When Peter denied Jesus

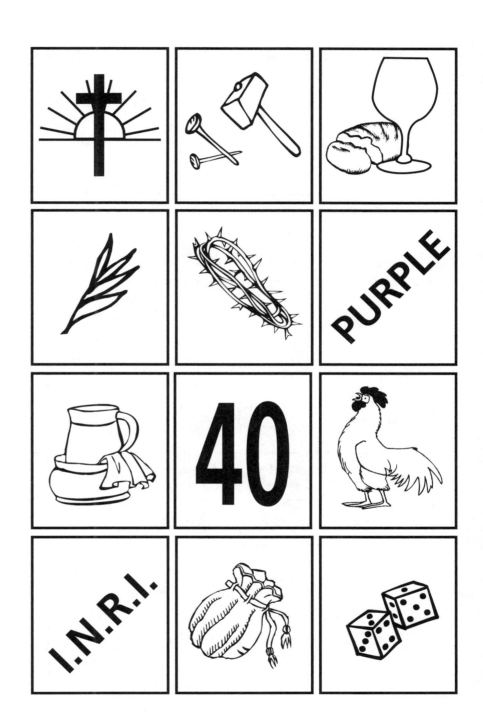

Color the answers

1. Who is the Redeemer?
2. What is another name for the feast of the Resurrection?
3. Who helped Jesus carry the cross?
4. What is the symbol of the death of Jesus?
5. What represents the Light of the risen Lord?
6. What reminder do we receive on the first day of Lent?
7. What word is used on Palm Sunday?
8. Who stood with John at the foot of the cross?
9. What is the nighttime celebration of the Resurrection called?
10. What night was Jesus captured in the garden?
11. What is blessed at the Easter Vigil?
12. What liturgical season prepares us for Easter?
13. What day commemorates Christ's death-burial?
14. What is a traditional way of doing penance?
15. What did people of Jerusalem wave?
16. Who denied Jesus three times?
17. Where was Christ crucified?
18. Who betrayed Jesus?
19. What do we call the "first Mass"?
20. What feast celebrates the exodus of the Israelites from Egypt?
21. Who pronounced the death sentence on Jesus?
22. What did Jesus wash for the disciples?
23. How long does Lent last?
24. Who did Jesus welcome into heaven?
25. Where did Jesus go to pray with his disciples?

		Jesus Christ	Cross	Good Friday		
		Stations	Ashes	Mount Sinai		
Garden of Olives	Tomb	Spear	Lent	John	Wine	Good Thief
Hosanna	Simon the Cyrene	Mount Calvary	Judas	Holy Thursday	Passover	Paschal Candle
Forty Days	Soldier	Robe	Mary	Advent	Eucharist	Palm Branches
		Baptism	Fasting	Dust		
		Nails	Easter	Four Weeks		
		Kiss	Pilate	Mark		
		Herod	Easter Vigil	Thorns		
		Hands	Peter	Holy Orders		
		Their Feet	New Fire	Last Supper		

The Last Supper

Church Teaching

Catechism of the Catholic Church, paragraphs 610–611, 1340–1341

Goals

To understand the role of the Passover in Jewish history

To learn how to be servants to others, care for others, as Jesus was for his disciples

To see the Last Supper as the time when Jesus asked us to remember him when we celebrate Mass

Supplies

Bible

Picture and crayons

Directions for Activities

- Read Exodus 12:1–14 and John 13:1–17. While these stories are being read, the child(ren) may color the picture of Jesus washing the feet of others.

  The Passover is a major feast for Jewish people. It celebrates how God saved the people and allowed them to escape from Egypt. It was at the feast of Passover that Jesus had a "last supper" with his followers. He washed their feet to show them that they should serve others as he served them. Then they shared a meal and he told them that when they eat the bread and drink the wine together to do it in memory of him for he is present with them.

- Fill in the list of people you can help, showing "love for one another as Jesus loved you."

"Love one another as I have loved you."

People I Can Help

Stations of the Cross

Church Teaching

Catechism of the Catholic Church, paragraphs 853, 1816

Goals

To learn the various stops on Jesus' journey to Calvary

To pray the stations together

To discover where the stations are located in your parish church

Supplies

Bible

Sheet of stations

Pencils, paper, crayons

Directions for Activities

- Read this section of the Passion story: Matthew 27:27–38.

- Take a copy of the fourteen stations. Read the stations and discuss the meaning of each.

- Choose one of the stations. Draw a picture as if this was happening today. Write a prayer about this station.

  Example: Station 2: "Jesus Takes Up His Cross": The cross is heavy. Can Jesus carry it? Dear Jesus, sometimes my problems seem too heavy for me. Give me the strength I need to do the hard things and to turn to you when I need help.

- Say this prayer together: "We adore you, O Christ, and we bless you, because by your holy cross you have redeemed the world."

The Fourteen Stations

1. Jesus is condemned to death.

2. Jesus bears his cross.

3. Jesus falls for the first time.

4. Jesus meets his mother.

5. Simon helps Jesus carry the cross.

6. Veronica wipes the face of Jesus.

7. Jesus falls a second time.

8. Jesus meets the women of Jerusalem.

9. Jesus falls a third time.

10. Jesus is stripped of his garments.

11. Jesus is nailed to the cross.

12. Jesus dies on the cross.

13. Jesus is taken down from the cross.

14. Jesus is placed in the tomb.

Christ the Light

Church Teaching

Catechism of the Catholic Church, paragraphs 1243, 1254

Goals

To hear the story of Jesus' resurrection at the Easter Vigil, the night before Easter

To understand that the Easter candle is a sign that Christ is the "Light of the World"

Supplies

Bible

Picture of Easter candle

Crayons or colored pencils

Directions for Activities

• Read 1 John 1:5–7.

• The Easter candle is lit at Mass during the Easter season as a sign that Christ is with us. It is always lit for baptisms and funerals and other special prayer times of the year.

• Take a copy of the Easter candle and note that it has a cross in the middle as a symbol of Jesus' death on the cross. It has an A at the top (for the Greek letter alpha, which means beginning) and and upside down U at the bottom (for the Greek letter omega, which means end). These two letters are symbols that Christ is everything to us, from the beginning of our lives to the end. The numbers show the year we are in. Color in the symbols on the Easter candle.

Easter Candle

Easter

Church Teaching

Catechism of the Catholic Church, paragraphs 647, 1168–1169

Goals

To celebrate the resurrection of Jesus

To understand that "new life" involves change and growth

To pray as a family for Easter joy and light

Supplies

Bible

Copies of the butterfly sheet

Explanation of the butterfly symbol

Crayons or markers

Directions for Activities

• Read John 20:1–9.

• As the caterpillar goes from cocoon to beautiful butterfly, so, we too go through changes in our lives until we will come to new life in God. Take a copy of the butterfly sheet, color the butterfly, and fold its wings back as a symbol of new life. Then say the prayer on it together as a family.

Dear Jesus,

Thank you for giving us new life through your resurrection.

May Easter be a time of light and joy for our family and may we work together to be your followers in all that we do.

We rejoice that you are with us always.

Amen.

Alleluia.

Learning Centers for
Intergenerational
Gatherings

No matter what form your parish faith formation takes, learning centers can be an effective part of the process. They provide a way for families to individualize their learning, pace it according to their own needs, and include their extended family members and members of the whole parish community in the process.

The learning centers recommended in this section of the book combine elements from the Advent or Lent centers arranged for four intergenerational gatherings. During Advent these can be the weekly gatherings for faith formation when the children would ordinarily gather or they can be experienced between Sunday Masses. However they are used, they involve families in the preparation for these seasons and encourage other adults in the parish to learn more about and share their faith.

Note that the sessions require a facilitator to do the following: set up the centers, lead the prayer and discussions, and generally provide a "process" for moving through the centers successfully.

Jesse Tree

Goal

Each of us has a family tree. Jesus also has a family tree, which we call the "Jesse tree." The goal of this session is to learn about the ancestors of Jesus and to make symbols for a Jesse tree.

Notes to Facilitator

Before participants arrive for this experience, set up a prayer area with the Bible enthroned. Also have a small Christmas tree (or an empty branch) ready. When all have arrived, light the candle(s) on the Advent wreath and invite one of the adults to proclaim the Word of God from Matthew 1:1–16 and Isaiah 11:1.

At the conclusion of the reading, invite persons or families to spend an amount of time drawing or listing the names of people they know who are part of their "family tree" (see page 7). Who in the group can recall the most distant relative?

Now have someone read about the meaning of the family tree of Jesus:

> The story we read at Christmas tells us that Jesus was the relative of King David, Israel's greatest King. And, going back even farther, part of his ancestry was Abraham, the father of the Hebrew nation. Through these and other faithful people, God took flesh as Jesus and lived among us. Our faithful ancestors/relatives have handed the faith on to us today. In Isaiah 11:1 we heard of the shoot coming forth from the root of Jesse, the father of David. This shoot, this person is Jesus. The stories of these and other ancestors of Jesus tell us how God chose, saved, and redeemed a people and made us adopted children belonging to the family of God in a special way.

- Divide the participants into groups of six to eight. Be sure there are some children in each group. Have them seated at a table. Now have each person draw the name of one of the ancestors of Jesus from a basket (see page 6).

- On each group table have a variety of art materials that can be used to make the symbol of the ancestor each chose. Each person should get the materials he or she will need.

- When all in the group have made a symbol, take time to do the activities on "The Church Year" (see page 11). The various seasons of the church year invite us to celebrate the events in the life of Jesus and in our own spiritual lives.

  When all are finished, sing "O Come, O Come Emmanuel" as each person takes his or her symbol and hangs it on the tree saying: "I bring a symbol of _____ who passed on the faith to us."

  When all have hung their symbols, say together: "Come, Lord Jesus, come and be our guest. Amen."

St. John the Baptist

Goal

St. John the Baptist prepared the way for his cousin, Jesus. He invited everyone to prepare the way of the Lord. We are still called to do this today.

Notes to Facilitator

Before participants arrive, set up a prayer space with the Bible enthroned and an Advent wreath. When they arrive, light the Advent candle(s) and invite one of the adults to proclaim the word of God from Luke 3:1–6.

- At the conclusion of the reading, divide the participants into groups of six to eight. Be sure there are some children in each group. Ask each group to discuss the following questions:

  » On our path to Christmas, John the Baptist reminds us to fill every valley and level every mountain in our lives to make the way straight and smooth for Jesus to enter our lives. What are some hills and valleys in your life?

  » How can you "prepare the way" for Jesus?

  » John the Baptist reminds us to wait for the Lord with patience. How can you practice patience in your life?

- Invite each group to complete three learning centers: "Prepare the Way for Jesus" (see page 16); "Be Watchful and Patient" (see page 19); and "Presents and Presence" (see page 21).

- When the groups have completed the activities, allow time for sharing what they experienced. Invite all to gather around the prayer space and pray the adapted version of the Benedictus below. This is the prayer that Zechariah, father of John the Baptist and husband of Elizabeth, sang to God in thanksgiving. Adults can take turns reading the prayer, and children can say the response: "Blessed be the Lord."

Reader One   Blessed be the Lord, the God of Israel who has come to us and set us free. God has raised up for us a mighty Savior born of the house of David. Through the holy prophets God promised to save us from our enemies, from the hands of all who hate us.

Response   Blessed be the Lord.

Reader Two   God promised to show mercy to our fathers and mothers and made a holy covenant with them. This was the oath God swore to our father Abraham, to set us free from the hands of our enemies, free to worship without fear, holy and righteous in God's sight all the days of our life.

Response   Blessed be the Lord.

Reader Three   You, my child, shall be called the prophet of the Most High for you will go before the Lord to prepare his way, to give to his people knowledge of their salvation by forgiving their sins. In the tender compassion of our God, the dawn from on high shall break upon us, to shine on those who dwell in darkness and the shadow of death, and to guide our feet on the road of peace (Luke 1:68–79).

Response   Blessed be the Lord.

Leader   Jesus Christ has begun a good work in us.
Jesus, please continue to help us be signs of your presence in the world today.

Leader   Jesus calls us to feed the hungry.
All   Help us to reach out to others.

Leader   Jesus calls us to visit the sick.
All   Help us to reach out to others.

Leader   Jesus calls us to visit those in prison.
All   Help us to reach out to others.

Leader   Jesus calls us to give drink to the thirsty.
All   Help us to reach out to others.

Leader   Jesus calls us to give shelter to the homeless.
All   Help us to reach out to others.

Leader   Jesus calls us to clothe the naked.
All   Help us to reach out to others.

Leader   O Lord, help us this Advent to do good things for all those in need, and to remember your words, "What you do for them, you do for me." Amen.

Names for Jesus

Goal

Jesus is known by many names including Prince of Peace and Light of the World. In this session, we will focus on the meaning of the names and celebrate them.

Notes to Facilitator

Before participants arrive, set up a prayer space with the Bible and an Advent wreath. When all have arrived, light the Advent candle(s) and invite one of the adult participants to proclaim the word of God from Mark 1:9–11.

- Divide the participants into groups of six to eight. Be sure there are children in each group. Invite the groups to complete activities at three learning centers: "The O Antiphons" (see page 8); "Names for Jesus" (see page 24); and "Jesus Gives Peace and Light" (see page 28).

- When the groups have completed the activities, allow time for sharing what they experienced. Ask them to discuss the following questions:

  When conflicts happen at home or school, what should you do?

  What happens when you blame others for things they didn't do?

  Who first told you about Jesus? What is your favorite name for Jesus? Why?

- When the discussion is finished, gather together for the following prayer:

Leader	Jesus is the light for the poor.
All	Help me be a light to the world.
Leader	Jesus is a light for children.
All	Help me be a light to the world.
Leader	Jesus is a light for those who are worried.
All	Help me be a light to the world.
Leader	Jesus is a light for those who are sad.
All	Help me be a light to the world.

Leader	Jesus is a light for the weary.
All	Help me be a light to the world.
Leader	Jesus is a light for people of faith.
All	Help me be a light to the world.
Leader	O Leader of Israel
All	Come, Lord Jesus!
Leader	O Wisdom
All	Come, Lord Jesus!
Leader	O Root of Jesse
All	Come, Lord Jesus!
Leader	O Key of David
All	Come, Lord Jesus!
Leader	O Rising Dawn
All	Come, Lord Jesus!
Leader	O King of Nations
All	Come, Lord Jesus!
Leader	O Emmanuel, God-with-us
All	Come, Lord Jesus!

Leader   O God, you show yourself to us in many ways and names. Help us to call on you and praise you forever. We ask this in Jesus' name. Amen.

(Ask participants to share a sign of peace.)

Mary and Joseph at Bethlehem

Goal

Mary was chosen to be the mother of Jesus; Joseph cared for Jesus and Mary. The goal of this session is to prepare for the coming of Jesus by loving and serving others.

Notes to Facilitator

Before participants arrive, set up a prayer space with the Bible enthroned and an Advent wreath displayed. When all have arrived, light the Advent candle(s) and invite one of the adults to proclaim the word of God from Luke 2:1–7. At the conclusion, all bow their heads and pray the "Hail Mary."

- Divide the participants into groups of six to eight. Be sure there is a child in each of the groups. Take some time to discuss the following questions:

    Imagine that you are Mary or Joseph. How are you feeling right now?

    How do you feel when you are chosen to do something special?

    Do you ask God's help when you are in need or worried?

- Now each take a sheet of paper and follow the directions to make a cut-and-fold crib with adults helping the children. The children can cut up some yellow strips of paper. Go around the room, asking each person to name something he or she can do to get ready for Christmas. Each time something is suggested, have children put a strip of yellow paper in the crib as "straw" (see page 36).

- Ask the groups to complete the activities at two learning centers: "Mary the Mother of Jesus" (see page 32) and "A Special Christmas Card" (see page 38). When completed, return to the group, do the matching game and answer the questions about Jesus.

- Pray as a group the adapted version of the Magnificat below, the prayer Mary said when she visited her cousin Elizabeth:

My soul proclaims your greatness, O God.
My spirit rejoices in you
    for you have looked with favor on your lowly servant,
    and from this day forward all generations
    will call me blessed.
You, O God, have done great things for me;
    holy is your name.
You have mercy on those who fear you
    in every generation.
You have shown the strength of your arm,
    you have scattered the proud in their conceit.
You have cast down the mighty from their thrones,
    and have lifted up the lowly.
You have filled the hungry with good things,
    and sent the rich away empty.
You have come to the help of your servant Israel
    for you have remembered your promise of mercy,
    the promise you made to our fathers and mothers,
    to Abraham and his children forever.

- Now take time to watch an Advent/Christmas video.

Prayer, Fasting, Almsgiving

Goal

To see Jesus as our guide for lenten prayer, fasting, and reaching out to those in need.

Notes to Facilitator

Before participants arrive, set up a prayer area with the enthroned Bible, a cross, and a candle (the Easter candle if it is available). When all have arrived, light the candle and invite one of the adults to proclaim the word of God from Joel 2:12–13, 15–16.

- Divide participants into groups of six to eight. Be sure there are children in every group. In each group, discuss ways that you can "turn on" to God during Lent. What can you do to deepen your prayer life, from what do you need to fast, and how can you reach out to those in need?

- At each group table, have the materials to explain and make pretzels ("A Reminder of Prayer," see page 54). When all have finished, place them on parchment paper with the person's name and bake them in an oven. When the pretzels are finished, groups complete the activities at three centers: "Lenten Practices" (see page 57); "A Holy Place" (see page 61); and "We Have Living Water" (see page 75).

When all have finished, gather for discussion about the activities, and then join hands and pray together the Our Father.

The Cross

Goal

To understand and appreciate the cross as a sign of being Christian.

Notes to Facilitator

Before participants arrive, set up a prayer space with the enthroned Bible, a cross, and a candle (Easter candle if possible). When all have arrived, light the candle, and invite one of the adults to proclaim the Word of God from John 3:16. Sing "Lift High the Cross."

- At the conclusion of the reading and song, divide the participants into groups of six to eight and complete the activities at "The Cross" (see page 44).

- When the group has completed the activities, allow time for sharing. Then talk about the fourteen stations of the cross ("Stations of the Cross," page 85) and how they could apply to situations today. Give each a piece of paper to draw an illustration of how one of the stations could be experienced by people today.

- After all have had sufficient time for this, gather in a large group. In the large group give all a copy of the fourteen stations of the cross ("Stations of the Cross," page 86). Slowly and reflectively take turns reading the title of each station. Respond to each station: "We adore you, O Christ, and we bless you, because by your holy cross you have redeemed the world."

A Time for Change

Goal

To understand that God's power in our lives can transform, transfigure, and change us.

Notes to Facilitator

Before participants arrive, set up a prayer area with the enthroned Bible, a cross, and a candle (Easter candle if it is available). When all arrive, light the candle, and invite an adult participant to proclaim the Word of God from Mark 9:2–10 and Genesis 15:5–18.

• After the reading, divide into groups of six to eight and discuss the following questions:

Abraham was called by God to be the father of the Jewish people. Abraham needed to be changed. How was his life going to change?

What is meant by descendants? From whom are you descended?

Who handed on your faith to you?

Can you imagine seeing Jesus in all his glory? How might you have responded?

• After the discussion, complete the activities at three centers: "Our Need for Change" (see page 63); "Jesus Gives Us Light" (see page 72); and "Jesus Blesses Us" (see page 66).

• Gather everyone to discuss how the faces on the sheet reveal their feelings. Invite participants to discuss these questions:

» Do our faces often show how we are thinking or feeling?

» Can we change the way we are feeling?

» How can we change bad feelings to good feelings?

» How can prayer help us to change?

After discussion, all gather for common prayer, taking a moment of silence between each phrase read by the leader:

Leader   Help us to change from being unforgiving to forgiving.
All   Lord be with us.

Leader	Help us to change from being lazy to being energetic.
All	Lord be with us.

Leader	Help us to change from lying to being truthful.
All	Lord be with us.

Leader	Help us to change from being mean spirited to being kind.
All	Lord be with us.

Leader	Help us to change from being stubborn to being open.
All	Lord be with us.

Leader	Help us to change from selfishness to generosity.
All	Lord be with us.

Leader	Help us to change from being disobedient to being obedient.
All	Lord be with us.

Leader	Please repeat after me "We are the glory of God, fully alive!"

Invite all to share a sign of peace before they leave.

Holy Week

Goal

During Holy Week we celebrate the passion, death, and Resurrection of Jesus, our life and our light.

Notes to Facilitator

Before participants arrive, set up a prayer area with the enthroned Bible, a candle, and the symbols used during Holy Week ("Symbols of Lent," page 80). Also have about twelve large bowls, water pitchers, and towels prepared. When all arrive, light the candle and ask an adult to proclaim the word of God from Mark 15:29—16:6 or John 13:2–17.

- Divide into groups of six to eight with some children in each group. In each group use the cross game—questions and answers—do this as a group until all the answers are found.

- Now have each group complete three centers: "Christ the Light" (page 87); "The Last Supper" (page 83); and "Easter" (page 89).

- When all the activities are completed, all gather together. Place the Easter candle in the center of the group. Take the several bowls for washing feet—adults and children take turns washing the feet of one another. As they do so say the words to each "Love one another as I have loved you."

Now each take the butterfly they made—the reminder of the Risen Christ—and holding them in the air say, "Jesus Christ is truly risen." Then all sing "Jesus Christ Is Risen Today."

Making Choices

Goal

To learn that prayer and study help us to make good choices and that Jesus comes to show us the way.

Notes to Facilitator

Before participants arrive, set up a prayer space with the enthroned Bible, a candle, and a cross. When all have arrived, light the candle, and invite an adult participant to read the word of God from John 8:1–11.

- Now divide into groups of six to eight. Be sure there are children in each group. Invite each group to complete the centers "Making Choices" (see page 47), "Jesus Gives Life" (see page 69), "Jesus Gives Us Light" (see page 72), and "Keeping the Commandments" (see page 51).

- When the group has completed the centers, gather together to review what they experienced from the various centers.

  Before departing, have all gather for prayer. Pray together the Guardian Angel prayer (see page 50).

Leader   Lord, you have promised to love us. Help us to follow your commandments so that we may grow in holiness by loving and caring for others. We pray this in Jesus' name. Amen.

Appendix

Letter to Parents for Advent

Notes to Facilitator

Have copies of this letter available for parents or guardians to read before they begin visiting the learning centers. Please feel free to add any additional information.

Dear Parents,

Thank you for taking this time to work with your children and other parish or family members as you anticipate the liturgical feast of Christmas. The four weeks of Advent help us to focus on the meaning of the coming of Christ, our Emmanuel.

These learning centers may be completed in any order you wish. A sheet with directions is provided at each center. It tells you the learning goals of each center for you and your child. It also gives directions for the activities. At each center you will also find a recommended reading from the *Catechism of the Catholic Church*, a suggested Scripture passage to share, plus the supplies you will need for the activities.

When you have finished at a center, please take your projects with you and leave the center in good order for the next family. To complete the activities at all of the learning centers will take approximately two hours. Please don't rush. Take all the time you need to share the Scripture readings and activities and answer any questions your child may have. If there are questions you need help with, please ask.

Here are the names and numbers for each center:

1. The Jesse Tree
2. O Antiphons
3. The Church Year
4. Prepare the Way for Jesus
5. Be Watchful and Patient
6. Presents and Presence
7. Names for Jesus

8. Jesus Gives Peace and Light
9. Mary the Mother of Jesus
10. St. Joseph
11. A Special Christmas Card
12. Bethlehem
13. Advent/Christmas Video

Thank you for spending this time with your child. My hope is that after you visit these centers, you will celebrate Advent and Christmas in more meaningful ways.

Letter to Parents for Lent

Notes to Facilitator

Have copies of this letter available for parents or guardians to read before they begin visiting the learning centers. Please feel free to add any additional information.

Dear Parents,

Thank you for taking this time during Lent to work with your children and other parish or family members as you anticipate the liturgical feast of Easter. The forty days of Lent invite us not only to turn away from sin but also to "turn on" to Jesus in our lives. They help us prepare more faithfully for the celebration of Easter in our homes and our hearts.

These learning centers can be completed in any order you wish. A sheet with directions is provided at each. This gives you the learning goals for you and your child. It also gives directions for the activities. At each center you will also find recommended readings from the *Catechism of the Catholic Church*, a suggested Scripture passage to share, plus the supplies you will need for the activities. When you have finished at a center, please take your projects with you and leave the center in good order for the next family. To complete the activities at all of the learning centers will take approximately two hours. Please don't rush. Take all the time you need to share the Scripture readings and activities and answer any questions your child may have. If there are questions you need help with, please ask.

Here are the names and numbers for each center:

1. The Cross	7. Our Need for Change
2. Making Choices	8. Jesus Blesses Us
3. Keeping the Commandments	9. Jesus Gives Life
4. A Reminder of Prayer	10. Jesus Gives Us Light
5. Lenten Practices	11. We Have Living Water
6. A Holy Place	12. Lent/Easter Video

Options for Holy Week

1. Symbols for Lent	4. Christ the Light
2. The Last Supper	5. Easter
3. Stations of Cross	

Thank you for spending this time with your child. My hope is that after you visit these centers, you will experience Easter as a season of peace, joy, and renewed faith.

Evaluation Form

Note to Facilitator

Have the form below available for parents to complete once they have visited all the learning centers with their child.

Parents, when you have visited all the learning centers, please complete this evaluation. Thank you.

The number of times I have participated in learning centers with this child: ____

In total I was able to spend: ____1 hour ____2 hours ____hours

Things my child and I found helpful (check all that apply):
____Having a place and time to adequately focus on the themes
____Spending quality time together
____Having the opportunity to talk about faith
____Having the supportive presence of other parents and children
____Other (please specify): _____

_____

Things my child and I found difficult with the centers (check all that apply):
____Scheduled days   ____Activities (explain): _____
____Time of day   ____Other (please specify): _____

Do you have any other comments about the use and value of the learning centers?

_____   _____
Your name   Date

_____

Gathering Prayer for Advent

If you gather with all participants before they visit the learning center, you can use this group prayer. In your prayer area, include an Advent wreath (or candle), a banner, and an enthroned Bible.

Leader   Let us prepare the way of the Lord.
All   Come, Lord Jesus.

Opening Song   "O Come, O Come Emmanuel"

Leader   Come, Lord Jesus, do not delay; give courage to your people. By your coming, help us to know the joy of your kingdom. We pray in your name. Amen.

Reading   Luke 1:26–37

Action   On the banner have the outline of an empty crib. Invite each child to cut a few strips of yellow paper (representing straw) to put into (paste onto) the crib.

(Explain that when they do good deeds for others, they are doing them for Jesus as well. The straw is a reminder of this.)

Leader   Jesus, you are Wisdom.
All   Come, Lord Jesus.

Leader   Jesus, you are Lord of Lords.
All   Come, Lord Jesus.

Leader   Jesus, you are the Root of Jesse.
All   Come, Lord Jesus.

Leader   Jesus, you are the Key of David.
All   Come, Lord Jesus.

Leader   Jesus, you are the Radiant Dawn.
All   Come, Lord Jesus.

Leader   Jesus, you are King of All Nations.
All   Come, Lord Jesus.

Leader   Jesus, you are Emmanuel, God-with-us.
All   Come Lord Jesus.

Pray together   Hail Mary, full of grace, the Lord is with you. Blessed are you among women and blessed is the fruit of your womb, Jesus. Holy Mary, Mother of God, pray for us sinners, now and at the hour of our death. Amen.

Families may now begin work at the various centers.

Gathering Prayer for Lent

If you gather with all participants before they visit the learnng centers, you can use this group prayer. In your prayer area, include an enthroned Bible, a cross, a candle, and a banner.

Leader	We adore you, O Christ, and we bless you.
All	Because by your holy cross you have redeemed the world.
Opening Song	"Jesus, Remember Me" (sing three times)
Leader	Loving God, may our acts of kindness during Lent bring us your mercy and love. Open our hearts to your love and prepare us for the coming feast of Easter. We ask this through Jesus who dwells with you and the Holy Spirit as one God.
All	Amen.
Reading	Matthew 26:36–44
Action	On the banner, have a large outline of a cross. Invite each child to write on a piece of paper something they will try to do to help others during Lent. Pin these on the cross outline.
Leader	Lord, help us open our hearts to you.
All	Create in us a new heart.
Leader	Lord, turn us toward you during Lent.
All	Create in us a new heart.
Leader	Lord, make us people of prayer.
All	Create in us a new heart.
Leader	Lord, help us listen to your Word.
All	Create in us a new heart.
Leader	Lord, forgive our sins.
All	Create in us a new heart.
Pray together	"Our Father, who art in heaven…."

Families may now begin work at the various centers.